OCCD–**Root** of the **Poisonous Tree**

*The **Psychological Disorder** at the Base of **Addiction**, **Alcoholism**, and **More***

Wolfgang **SCHULTZ**

outskirts press

Preface

Thank you for showing interest in something that can change the very way we look at addiction, alcoholism, and other social issues. This book was written to give people who may not be educated in psychology or had experience in what an addict or alcoholic goes through.

This book is about Obsessive Compulsive Control Disorder (OCCD), and will help you understand how a person thinks and what actions are consistent with this disorder. The first three chapters are how this disorder was discovered and how it was isolated and defined. Chapter four actually explains what it is in clinical terms.

The chapters that follow will show its impact on society, and how it can be seen in various other social problems such as Bulling, Domestic Violence, and Teen Suicide.

It was some work to put this together. I spent twelve years in the research and identification on this disorder. Then I wrote the book, after I offered to share this information with the psychological community at various colleges and universities.

I hope you enjoy read it and hope that it will answer some questions you might have about people in your life.

To all those who have helped me understand this, I say thank you from the bottom of my heart! I hope not only that I have given you something back, but can also help you further with this book.

Table of Contents

CHAPTER 1

The Discovery

Oddly enough, this all starts out with Professional Wrestling. I have been a pro wrestler for over twenty years. I've been all over the globe and met quite a few wrestlers along the way. It's been a fun ride, but nothing like you would think it to be.

Wrestling has been quite costly. Anyone who has seriously done it will tell you. I have one divorce, and I've lost count on how many girlfriends came and went. That would be on top of the pains and injuries you get. Many wrestlers get addicted to pain medications. I was lucky enough not to mess with it.

I remember when I first started out, an old timer told me to get involved in charitable activities. Working with communities, and working with kids. He told me promoters like to see that on your resume. Getting a promoter's attention is how you get work in the ring and get in front of crowds. I thought it was a good idea, so I got involved.

I had a manager, Tom Howard. He set up a few hospital visits with the kids for me. I remember the first time I visited a hospital, I felt guilty. I think I got more out it than the kids did. I was told that's how it works. The old timer told me that was God's reward for doing good.

I expanded out into other venues. I hosted a health fair, and started visiting schools. It's really something when the little kids hang on your every word, and the bigger kids start feeling more confident because they could talk to you, one on one.

I was contacted by a high school teacher in 2005. She had heard I had been to various schools and wondered if I could give a talk about the dangers of Performance Enhancing Drugs (PEDs). She told me high school students were using them to bulk up to get a scholarship. She was concerned about the long-term effect.

I told her I would have to do some research on it. I will never name names because I always made it a point to leave when I thought someone was going to use them. I personally never witnessed anyone using them, but I did know somethings about them.

I wanted this to be informative as well as inspirational. I wanted to start out showing them they were wasting their time with PED's. There are so many other ways to improve your athletic performance. I created a program called "A Better Athlete in 5 Minutes". There is clearly too much emphasis on size and strength. There are other things that will get you playing time and no one seems to talk about it. There are also areas coaches seem to miss when they are preparing their athletes. My goal is to show every kid they have a chance to play and play well.

As I was looking at the presentation, I tried to think of the questions I might get. Some of the wrestling questions are pretty standard, so I was ready for those. One question I thought I might get would be a stumper. If a kid asked "Are they addictive?" No one has an answer to that! So many athletes deny they used them when they really did, and the ones who got caught on a drug screen won't talk about them. The ones who tested dirty all say it was a one-time thing.

So, before I could get in front of these kids, I really needed to at least understand the elements of an addiction and how it affected someone. I did a search on the internet and found several programs. The one I found that was easiest to find was Alcoholics Anonymous (AA). I decided it would be quicker and easier to go to a meeting or two of AA to get my answer. Boy was I wrong!

The first meeting I went to, there were over 30 men and no women; even though the meeting was open to women. The chairperson asked if anyone had never been to a meeting before, so I raised my hand, Big Mistake! They went around the room telling their life stories about drinking. They kept giving me coffee and after an hour and a half the meeting ended and then they told me where the bathroom was.

I learned something unique while I listened to them. The ones who talked about how old they were when they started all fell into 11 to 16 years of age bracket. What no one seemed to know is that all your life long habits are established in your first 16 years of your life, like how to make a sandwich and how you wipe your bottom. I saw this as a point I could use when talking to high school students, but I still didn't know what elements made an addict.

I kept going to more meetings and made it a point to go early. It gave me a chance to pick the brains of some of the old timers. As I went to more meetings. I found out how imposing the court system is on the AA meetings and the people who attend the fellowship. Most of the people who the court ordered to attend were there because of a drunken driving charge. Some were there for drug charges (not sure why the courts sent them to an alcohol treatment group), and some were on parole.

Now diversity is a good thing, but this kind of diversity was also a disruptive thing. When more than half the people in the room just want to get their court paper signed, it doesn't hold well for the content of the discussion. There were also people coming in thinking it was a talk therapy session and would tell all their problems to everyone in the group. Then these same people would get upset if someone said something about what they said to someone outside the group. It could be rather dysfunctional, but sometimes the old timers would make it worthwhile.

I also learned the difference between professional treatment and self-help treatment. The first two steps are the same, admit you have a problem and get help. The third is where there is the fork in the road. The professional treatment is to find out what made you drink in the first place, and the self-help was to believe that a higher power will watch over your life while you are fixing it.

AA itself was something amazing. It was created in 1940, just after prohibition had been repealed. Back then, mental illness meant you had to be locked up and treated in an institution. So, for AA to convince anyone that alcoholism was a mental illness, and that it could be treated outside an institution, was remarkable. Then again, they were talking to judges who had no place to send these "town drunks" and were tired of seeing them every Monday morning.

As I kept going to meetings, I learned there were two kinds of old timers. Those who, after completing the 12 steps, would look in the history of the program, and those who didn't care, as long as it worked. Not every old timer was a sponsor. A sponsor is someone who helps guide a newcomer in the program and the 12 steps. The court slip people would always look for a sponsor. Not that they were going to work on the 12 steps, but for someone to write a letter on their behalf so they could get their driver's license back.

I had many conversations, both with old timers and newcomers. Before the meetings, it's a lot like hanging out in a neighborhood bar. There are people talking about the weather, politics, sports, etc. There are also jokes and people getting picked on.

As I listened both in the meetings and outside of them, was something not just about alcohol or drugs. There was a different mindset that was very noticeable with the newcomers and somewhat with the old timers. In the old timers, it was more in reflection of how they were. There were some who fall into a third category. These people would drop in and out as their money and social circumstances would dictate. They would want credit for the time they put in the AA program, but they never stuck with it long enough to see the results.

I began to notice there was something about the 12 steps themselves. The way they were written, seemed to allude to something more than what was there. I did a little research and found out the steps were written and then authenticated by the first 100 people who worked through them. The point was to make sure each word said exactly what they meant. Nothing was unintentional in the steps and they also knew others would come along and add to what they have written. To say there is another mental illness underneath alcoholism or drug addiction in 1940 would have met with a lot of disbelief. Yet they do outline something within the 12 steps.

I believed I had found out what that hidden finding was. Now I went out to test the theory. I spoke privately with over 1500 people and attended over 2500 meetings. It was there that I had found the proof I needed and is what this book is about. As you read, you will see not only why this illness exists, but also how and where in the AA doctrine it is.

The real discovery comes in not what high are they chasing, but why that high means so much to them. Historically, treatment is based on the addiction to the substance, and the thrill of the high was assumed to be the motivator. However, if the motivator could be something deeper, it would explain how treatments of every kind fall short and why there are so many relapses.

With Alcoholics, drinking is more of a social activity. Drunkenness would be a byproduct of that. They do however see an abnormality in their consumption. They then gravitate to those who drink as much, or more than they do. They then look like one of the crowd, and not a person with a problem.

With the Addict, they would tend to also be in love with the first high they ever had from the substance. They "Chase the Dragon" and try more and also add combinations to their routine to get that same feeling as the first time. As with the Alcoholic, they too look for those who use like they do so as not to feel that they have a problem.

With both, they experience a psychological shift. The psyche was previously shifted, and with the substance, it makes a greater, more pronounced shift that must be looked at.

CHAPTER 2

Narrowing It Down

This is what lies under the exterior. It is what makes alcoholics and drug addicts act the way they do while not under the influence. As people who have lived with someone affected will tell you, a person's actions are different from their normal self and sometimes this behavior can be taught to their children. Before I or anyone else can label something a disorder, we have to explore what is already acknowledged as a disorder to be sure we have something that is truly unique. This is why we will look at some similar disorders while defining this one.

Obsessive Compulsive Control Disorder (OCCD), is a misalignment of the psyche, where a person lives through their Alter Ego (Latin for other self), instead of the Ego (Latin for self). This causes a personality change where the person is more aggressive or self-centered, and on the other side can feel victimized or helpless.

The key word is **control.** Many children of alcoholics and addicts can tell you that one or more parents were controlling.

They grew up in a home feeling weak and living in fear. This would be the effects of drugs and alcohol after the fact. From my research, it takes between three to four months for this neurosis to wear off.

It actually starts with the first state of intoxication. The psyche is knocked out of alignment (see diagram 1.1) The Ego, the part of your psyche that is the true you, and the Alter Ego, the part of your psyche that is everything you want to be or be recognized for, share space in the frontal lobe see diagram 1.2). Behind the Alter Ego is the Id, the part of the psyche that wants gratification at all costs. In a well aligned psyche, the Ego would be in the frontal lobe, with the Alter Ego behind it, and the Id behind the Alter Ego.

Because of this misalignment, the Ego and Alter Ego get into conflict and it produces what many people call a Jeckel & Hyde, referring to Dr. Jeckel and Mr. Hyde. As the habit develops to be more dominant, this misalignment becomes more prominent. It is why people with an addiction can't sleep. The Ego and Alter Ego get into a shouting match causing the brain to race to catch up.

From the Alter Ego we get the dominance, or urge for control. Of course, the Alter Ego has the confidence that it will get control and not be stopped by anyone or anything. From the Alter Ego we also get cunning. It will find ways to use and manipulate people to get what they want and get others to do the things they don't want to do. It can change quickly from dominance to cunning. In the AA reading How It Works, it describes alcohol as "Cunning, baffling, and powerful". Clearly this phase fits the workings of the Alter Ego.

Frontal Lobe

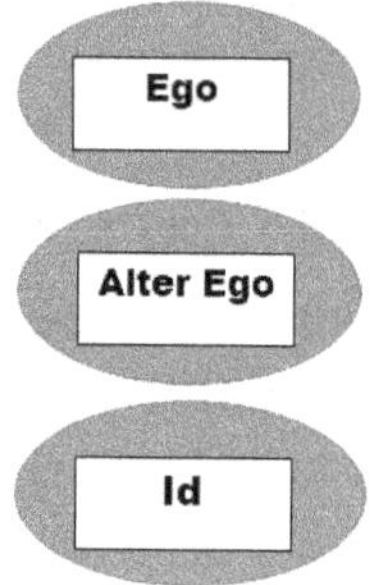

Normal Psyche Diagram 1.1

Frontal Lobe

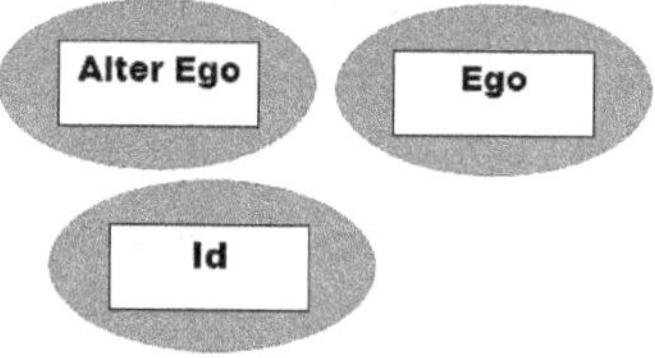

Alcoholic/Addict Psyche Diagram 1.2

From here, we will do some side-by-side comparisons within the American Psychiatric Association's book of all recognized disorders titled DSM-5. I will be **bold printing** anything from that book. The plain print would be my findings and how it relates.

Within the DSM-5, from the American Psychiatric Association, it describes a psychological disorder as:

A mental disorder is characterized by clinically significant disturbance in an individual's cognition, emotion, regulation, or behavior that reflects a dysfunction in the psychological, biological, or developmental processes underlying mental functioning. Mental disorders are usually associated with significant distress or disability in social, occupational, or other important activities. An expectable or culturally response to a common stressor or loss, such as death of a loved one, is not a mental disorder. Socially deviant behavior (e.g. political, religious, or sexual) and conflicts that are primarily between the individual and society are not mental disorders unless the deviance or conflict results from a dysfunction in the individual, as described above.

Going down the DSM-5 guidelines for Obsessive Compulsive Disorder (OCD), I will show how this diagnosis is more direct and on point than others have been. The basis for this is the motive behind the behavior, the motive being control.

Obsessions:

1. **Recurrent and persistent thoughts, urges, or images that are experienced, at some point during the disturbance, as intrusive, and unwanted, and that in most individuals causes marked anxiety or distress;**

You can easily see this on the surface with an alcoholic/addict when they first start treatment. However, this is present while they are still using. They feel unable to function without first getting a feeling of control.

The substance of choice puts them in a secure mental state by stimulating the Alter Ego. They experience a certain level of anxiety when looking into a mirror. The mirror can either show them the person they believe themselves to be (Alter Ego) or who they really are (Ego). Not really knowing keeps them away from mirrors.

Their thoughts will range from past, to future. They will not focus on the present until they first reconcile errors from the past, and see a glorious future. Only then will they seek to plan out the present.

When they then focus on the present, they are more interested on what others think of them. They become more co-dependent as their social circle shrinks but, to the World, they are what the Alter Ego says they are. It's here, where they are to impose their will and make people, places, and things to be what they want them to be.

2. **The individual attempts to ignore or suppress such thoughts, urges, or images, or to neutralize them with some other thought or action (i.e., performing a compulsion)**

The compulsions for OCCD would be a little different than with OCD. Much of the compulsions are directed to confirm their perfection they have established, or to use their control they have gained over others.

Again, this is a motive-based illness. It's also one that has a great deal of personal investment. Some of the compulsions would involve their parents, as in how to be different so they will not make the same mistakes. It is also a way of breaking control they feel someone has over them.

Self-pity is a thought pattern that fits here. They love nothing more than to know how people would feel sorry for the way they treated them. How the World would be a darker place without them. This thought pattern can only exist while they are not under any immediate threat.

Compulsions:

3. **Repetitive behaviors (e.g. hand washing, ordering, checking) or mental acts (e.g. praying, counting, repeating words silently) that the individual feels driven to perform in response to an obsession or rules that must be applied rigidly.**

Many of these compulsions are developed at a young age, if they grew up in a home with a person who has a drinking or drug problem. The alcoholic/addict would be very dominant and create nervous energy for others in the household. When they have fear and anxiety, with no place to hide, and nowhere to run to, the best defense is to look busy. Compulsive behavior for OCCD could also include wiping, sweeping, and other forms of cleaning.

As they develop into adulthood, the compulsions would have a direct link to control or power. Many will mentally repeat in their minds past events looking for better outcomes. This could last anywhere from a couple of minutes to over an hour.

Those with OCCD are also very territorial, in that they are

overly possessive over areas and objects, either they own, or responsible for, or feel they have a right to. This possessiveness can create irritability and cause outbursts of rage and anger for no apparent reason.

4. The behavior or mental acts are aimed at preventing or reducing anxiety or distress, preventing some dreaded event or situation; however, these behaviors or mental acts are not connected in a realistic way with what they are designed to neutralize or prevent, or are clearly excessive.

People with OCCD are emotional in the sense they are melodramatic. Every situation is a dire one and they are always in the middle of it, usually as the victim. They have a greater sense of self and it requires attention.

It is the greater sense of self that makes them want a World that matches their mood. If they are sad about having a disappointment, then the World should be a sad place. Instead of addressing the reason for the sadness, they instead will put people around them in a depressing situation.

They are however very good at blending in. They will often times mask their true feelings to be a part of a group or to get someone attention when their real mood comes out. They can be master manipulators when it comes to problems and people's effort when confronted with a problem.

People with OCCD will also take other people's problems. Sometimes it is to be seen as a great helper and good person. Other times it is because they feel they have to, from another person who also has OCCD. They are put into a guilt situation and feel obligated to take the problem.

Two key words that seem to attract them are "Drama" and "Trauma". They love the emotional playground. It gives them an audience and purpose from which to show themselves. It is also likely where they spent most of their time while growing up.

Within the DSM-5, in does mention Substance/Medication-Induced Obsessive-Compulsive or Related Disorder. This would be a description of bad episodes while under the influence and reactions to rehab and withdraw.

CHAPTER 3

OCCD Comparative to Other Personality Disorders

Again, we will do a comparative to something in the DSM-5. This disorder is very similar; however, it does have some vast differences. More than likely you can see why this could easily apply to someone you know with a substance abuse problem. Under the influence, this could look exactly alike.

There is a sharp contrast as I will show. First, the person with a substance abuse problem will seem to be a fit for these, while under the influence, because of the expansion of Ego that happens. A Narcissistic person is generally seen as egotistical; thus, the appearance is seen as the same. However, when a person comes down or out of the intoxication, their psyche will revert to more of a normal setting.

The differences are first, a person with OCCD is motivated

by control. They are either trying to escape someone else's control or gain control for themselves. The second is that a person with OCCD can see a line between their Ego and Alter Ego. As you have read earlier, these two will both try to be in charge of the frontal lobe, or thinking part of the brain. A person with Narcissistic Personality Disorder is trying to blend the Ego and Alter Ego, so as to not see where one stops and the other begins. We will go down the description from the DSM-5 and do a comparison.

Narcissistic Personality Disorder 301.81

A pervasive pattern grandiosity (in fantasy or behavior), need for admiration, and lack of empathy, beginning by early adulthood and present in a variety of contexts, as indicated by 5 (or more) of the following:

1. **Has a grandiose sense of self-importance (e.g., exaggerates achievements and talents, expects to be recognized as superior without consummate achievements).**

The term "Grandiose" refers to a heightened sense of self. Clearly, it would fit the person under the influence. When you look at the phrase as a whole, you will notice it also refers to past and future. It refers to deeds by talents gained before and respect for it in the future. What about the present? That is where it is fill-in-the-blank. The Egotistical statements cover up no effort or planned effort by the person.

Those with a substance abuse problem will often plan big. Then before they even start, already begin thinking how great it will be when it's done. All the respect they will get, what a nice job they did, and how they overcame all obstacles. Then they come down or sober up and realize that it is a huge project and they have no idea where to begin. It is the enjoyment of what they see themselves as that is the reason for this. But again, they know who they are and know what they can do. It would also be the reason for getting others to do the actual work. Then they can claim what a great job they did planning and organizing.

2. **Is preoccupied with fantasies of unlimited success, power, brilliance, beauty, or ideal love.**

An OCCD person, if not under the influence, a person would be more trying to figure out what they claimed while under the influence. The preoccupation would be damage control. They would want to make others think they were all of the above. They would also "Mask", a term for putting a public face on and not letting others see what is really going on.

In fantasies, they would be more about past event. The three magic words would be Should of, Would of, and Could of. Anything in their past that they can attach those words to, they will first review the events looking for the best spin and then what if they had a do over? How would that turn out?

3. **Believes that he or she is special and unique and can only be understood by, or should associate with, other special and high-status people (or institutions).**

Here is where it gets interesting for OCCD people. Many also deal with some depressive issues that would make them more introverted (not out-going). If they are indulging in drugs or alcohol, they will get past the introversion, but will find themselves losing ground in main stream society. Basically, the only people who will put up with them are others like them. Even that can be problematic at times.

In the maladjusted psyche, diagram 1-2, they will think they deserve better and will think they are worth more than those around them. They will also make it difficult for those whom they don't see as equals and look down on. They will compare themselves as equals to the elite people, but will never get close enough to say hello.

4. Requires excessive admiration.

OCCD people aren't looking for admiration, but they are looking for attention, sympathy, and empathy. They love the attention and will talk slowly and explain every detail in a story, if detail is needed or not. It really depends on what the person sees themselves as. When they see themselves as a social butterfly, or belle of the ball, they are more prone to require attention. Some of the other types will want attention only under certain circumstances.

5. Has a sense of entitlement (i.e., unreasonable expectations of especially favorable treatment or automatic compliance with his or her expectations).

In the AA 12 step program, they address expectations and entitlements. They address them as reasons for someone to get intoxicated. Clearly you can set yourself up for failure in expecting people to do everything you tell them or getting everything, you are entitled to.

It sets up a good against bad situation. Good that you get what you want but bad that you have to wait for it. To add also timeliness to your expectations would be imposing your will on others, or a type of control. One big difference is NPD is about gaining control, and OCCD is about having control.

6. Is interpersonally exploitive (i.e., takes advantage of others to achieve his or her own ends).

This would be a person pushing buttons to find a weakness, and then taking advantage of it. For many that weakness is fear, and for others it is ego. Every person has a weakness, but not every person is a slave to it.

Clearly a person with NPD would be using people for personal gain alone. A person with OCCD would be using them and trying to maintain a control on them for a later purpose. The more people an OCCD person has at their disposal, the more powerful they feel they are.

With an NPD person, it could be as much for amusement as it would be for personal gain. They believe that people and the World owes them and they are just collecting what is due.

7. Lacks empathy: is unwilling to recognize or identify with the feelings and needs of others.

This is one that is clearly an NPD symptom. With OCCD,

they have a need to show what a kind and caring person they are, in front of a group, of course. It feeds their alter ego to live within it for even a few minutes.

An NPD person feels they are the most important person in the World, so others only matter in how they fit them in their lives. They would not have a need to feed their alter ego since they are living from it.

8. Is often envious of others or believes others are envious of him or her.

This also is not consistent with OCCD. Depending if they are intoxicated, in that state, and ego rush could make them believe they are the envy of many. They themselves would not be envious. Those with OCCD not using intoxicants would not be affected, one way or the other.

9. Shows arrogant, haughty behaviors or attitudes.

When under the influence this would be a good description of an OCCD person. However, for a different reason than for an NPD person. An OCCD person would use this to justify why they don't have the friends they use to have. It would also excuse them from being well liked.

An NPD person would do this more for the entertainment value. To feel greater than others and creating reasons for it. It also creates a reason to be rude and obnoxious and have them feel no regrets. Again, it depends largely as to what is in their Alter Ego.

Histrionic Personality Disorder 301.50

A pervasive pattern excessive emotionally and attention seeking, beginning by early adulthood and present in a variety of contexts, as indicated by five (or more) of the following:

1. **Is uncomfortable in situations in which he or she is not the center of attention.**

Clearly an OCCD person wants fame, for everyone to know them and to acknowledge them. Being the center of attention with an agenda. They would be more likely to impose their will and mood upon others (i.e., if they are not happy, the World should be an unhappy place).

A Histrionic Personality Disorder (HPD) person would crave the attention for the sake of the attention. They would be more likely to adapt their actions to whatever mood the group was in. As long as people were watching and remained watching.

2. **Interaction with others is often characterized by inappropriate sexually seductive or provocative behavior.**

For an HPD person, any attention is good attention. It also gratifies their Ego to see themselves as desirable and someone who can get a rise out of others.

With an OCCD person, this would depend on if they were under the influence (passive or aggressive). In an aggressive mindset, it wouldn't be simple flirtation. There would be an agenda behind their actions.

3. Displays rapidly shifting and shallow expressions of emotions.

For an OCCD person, this would be for a feeling out process. How much is the conversation about them and how favorable is it. It's also a technique to find hot buttons in others. What is important to them and how much does it mean.

For an HPD person, it would all be about how much of a conversation was about them and how much wasn't.

4. Consistently uses physical appearance to draw attention to self.

It's all about getting attention. It can be looking good to wearing something strange or not within their normal wardrobe. Getting a reaction is the goal.

It clearly shows a lack of self-confidence and also self-respect, in some cases. In OCCD, it is not a consistent trait but, it is a common one.

5. Has a style of speech that is excessively, impressionistic, and lacking in detail.

Again, the objective is attention. When telling stories about experiences, they use dramatic pauses. Every detail given is self-serving. "Impressionistic" has to do with being theatrical. When they speak, they are giving a performance.

In OCCD, being theatrical is about hunting for and using a person's hot buttons, something they can gain advantage of to get someone to feel sorry for them or to keep them under their control. It is a way to also show themselves to be power-ful. Even if they are not.

6. Shows self-dramatization, theatricality, and exag-gerated expression of emotion.

This would be a way to keep the attention of them or to get the attention from a group away from another person. To stand out in a group or crowd.

In OCCD, it is used to further their point and gain their ad-vantage. Raising their voice doesn't go as far as some well-played theatrics. This is used more in the aggressive than the passive, but both will use it as a manipulation tool.

7. Is suggestable (i.e., easily influenced by others or circumstances).

Used as a way of showing their self-importance. Showing them to be leaders in what a person or group might say is important.

In OCCD, this isn't quite so common, unless there is an audi-ence to watch. It is used more as a way to win over others, and get favor.

8. Considers relationships to be more intimate than they actually are.

Showing their importance to others by using others. As long as they can show their importance in relation to them.

In OCCD, they are generally lonely and have difficulty being intimate with others. In a passive sense, it would be looking for a sense of belonging without feeling controlled. In the aggressive sense, it would be more ego building, a way to prove to themselves who they are and what they have in their lives.

Avoidant Personality Disorder 301.82

A pervasive pattern of social inhibition, feelings of inadequacy, and hypersensitivity negative evaluation, beginning by early adulthood and present in a variety of contexts, as indicated by four (or more) of the following:

1. **Avoids occupational activities that involve a significant interpersonal contact because of fears of criticism, disapproval, or rejection.**

Feelings of inadequacy in their career would leave them not wanting to hear and criticism about their work or work habits. This could also be a fear of talking about their personal life, or lack of.

In OCCD, it would apply more to the passive than the aggressive. A passive person can be very private and so reluctant to show others things about their lives that would also lend itself to their professional life as well. They are also trying to avoid depression and depressive thoughts, blaming themselves for whatever negativity might come up.

2. Is unwilling to get involved with people unless certain of being liked.

This is a way to avoid social rejection. That fear would be a reason for this behavior.

In OCCD Passive, the fear is coupled with a low self-esteem, created by a controlling person. This would be a symptom of someone with limited social opportunities.

3. Shows restraint within intimate relationships because of the fear of being shamed or ridiculed.

This would result in managing two people, the one they show the World, and the one beneath that. It's that inner person that has no defenses of experiences to draw upon.

In OCCD Passive, there is the above fears as well as the fear of when will reality strike. When will this end in yet another disappointment and how will they deal with it? Cinderella at the stroke of midnight feeling.

4. Is preoccupied with being criticized or rejected in social situations.

One burned, twice shy. The feelings of fear about the unknown and the lack of how to predict how things will turn out.

In OCCD Passive, they can predict when and where it will happen. The only unknown would be either an appearance of the controller or the controller coming up in conversation. When the controller isn't there, there is the fear of what the controller will be told later.

5. Is inhibited in new interpersonal situations because of feelings of inadequacy.

They live in the known, and fear the unknown. The awkwardness of meeting new people in a strange setting is too much to handle.

In OCCD Passive, it more hinges on the approval of the controller. If they feel the controller would not approve, then this would apply, if the controller would approve, then this wouldn't be a problem.

6. Views self as socially inept, personally unappealing, or inferior to others.

Generally speaking, this is what would happen when low self-esteem meets depression.

In OCCD Passive, this would be directly linked to the controller. These are tools controllers use to keep someone in a certain status of life. Controllers hate change unless they create it, so when a person experiences normal personal growth, they counter it with negative comments direct at the growth, and any good feelings associated with it.

7. Is unusually reluctant to take personal risks or to engage in any new activities because they may prove embarrassing.

This would be a suppression of the Alter Ego. Normal growth

requires us to try new things and to take some measure of risk.

In OCCD passive, this wouldn't appear as often. They would generally feel they had no time to pursue a new activity or risk. OCCD aggressive would be more effected by this because they generally lack the ability to laugh at themselves. They feel weakness when failure occurs.

Borderline Personality Disorder 301.83

A pervasive pattern of instability of interpersonal relationships, self-image, and affects, and marked impulsivity, beginning by early adulthood and present in a variety of contexts, as indicated by five (or more) of the following:

1. **Frantic efforts to avoid real or imagined abandonment. (Note: Do not include suicidal or self-mutilating behavior covered in Criterion 5.)**

In Borderline Personality Disorder (BPD), this would be a symptom of an instable self-esteem. The "frantic" part would indicate a lost sense of balance, between reality and perception.

In OCCD, this would occur in a person who is trying to show the public one side of their personality, and hide the true side of their personality. The term would be masking; an effort to hide the true self. The "abandonment" would be a sign of failure and thus create a frantic effort.

2. **A pattern of unstable and intense interpersonal relationships characterized by alternating between extremes of idealization and devaluation.**

In BPD, this would be a result of the underlining issues.

In OCCD, this would be the conflict resulting from the masking, if to show the true self or to continue using the mask. Rejection can be devastating, so the OCCD person will likely not have the final say in how the relationship would proceed. The main factors being ego, people pleasing, and depression.

3. **Identity disturbance: markedly and persistently unstable self-image or sense of self.**

In BPD, this would be very common. They would be trying to identify themselves in a wide range of parameters.

In OCCD, again, the battle between ego and people pleasing, to continue masking or reveal themselves.

4. **Impulsivity in at least two areas that are potentially self-damaging (e. g., spending, sex, substance abuse, reckless driving, binge eating). (Note: Do not include suicidal or self-mutilating behavior included in Criterion 5.)**

This would be a critical difference. In BPD, the efforts would be for thrills and also based on a hatred of self. "Potentially" self-damaging is the critical part of this, this would be a calculated risk.

In OCCD, the substance abuse would be a mainstay. If other forms appeared, they would not be used to self-damage as much to live within the Alter Ego. To please themselves within the Id, where anything goes as long as they can feel a satisfaction from it.

5. **Recurrent suicidal behavior, gestures, or threats, or self-mutilating behavior.**

In BPD, this would be either a call for help or attention, or an act of self-hatred.

In OCCD, this would be a sign of forfeiture, giving up. A depression would be present and the person wouldn't likely understand why they had these feelings, but more the reasoning they deserve what they were getting from it.

6. **Affective instability to a marked reactivity of mood (e.g., intense episodic dysphoria, irritability, anxiety usually lasting a few hours and only rarely more than a few days).**

In BPD, it would be a part of the underlining issue.

In OCCD, it would be an unusual symptom, unless it was a part of a depressive disorder.

7. **Chronic feelings of emptiness.**

In BPD, it would be part of the underlining issue.

In OCCD, it would be a familiar feeling. When in childhood, if they disappointed the adult alcoholic/addict, this would be how they would be made to feel. As an adult, the feeling would be a known and accepted feeling, and would not be uncommon enough to mention to anyone.

8. **Inappropriate, intense anger or difficulty controlling anger (e.g., frequent displays of temper, constant anger, recurrent physical fights).**

In BPD, the fight against the issue at hand. They would be struggling to feel something as opposed to feeling nothing.

In OCCD, this again would go back to their childhood. Anger is not to controlled; it is used to gain control. It is a survival trait.

9. **Transient, stress-related paranoid ideation or severe dissociative symptoms.**

In BPD, the feeling of being on both sides of an equation leaves them without a feeling of being on either side.

In OCCD, this would not be a symptom.

Obsessive-Compulsive Personality Disorder 301.4

A pervasive pattern of preoccupation with orderliness, perfectionism, and mental and interpersonal control, at the expense of flexibility, openness, and efficiency, beginning by early adulthood and present in a variety of contexts, as indicated by four (or more) of the following:

1. **Is preoccupied with details, rules, lists, order, organization, or schedules to the extent that the major point of the activity is lost.**

With Obsessive-Compulsive Personality Disorder (OCPD), the Obsession is detail and the compulsion would be perfection. The result is unimportant to the method that is used to gain it.

In OCCD, this is usually premeditated. The idea is to control the activity and keep the activity running on their schedule. Any point would be optional, as long as control was never lost.

2. **Shows perfectionism that interferes with task completion (e.g., is unable to complete a project because his or her own overly strict standards are not met).**

Again, in OCPD, the method is what matters most.

For OCCD, this would be an over-reach. Every addict/alcoholic is a perfectionist; however, the level is not dictated by an activity, rather by how much control they have within it.

3. **Is excessively devoted to work and productivity to the exclusion of leisure activities and friendships (not accounted for by obvious economic necessity).**

In OCPD, this would allow and excuse someone from manners and social niceties. This would be more common in a loner type.

In OCCD, this would primarily be seen more from greed. It can also be used for instilling a boost to the Ego. It would be more used as proof of importance to others without making claims, however, these efforts, if they were to go unnoticed, would cause an outburst.

4. **Is over conscientious, scrupulous, and inflexible about matters of morality, ethics, or values (not accounted for by cultural or religious identification).**

With OCPD, this would be a result of the person believing there is only black and white, there is no shades of grey. Life is absolute once they have found an identity in it.

In OCCD, this would be more consistent to most things as they relate to most people, however, there would be exceptions to certain people in certain circumstances. As each person in their life has a place and everyone must remain in their place unless given permission to leave that place.

5. **Is unable to discard worn-out or worthless objects even when they have no sentimental value.**

In OCPD, this would be hoarding, a symptom also in OCD.

In OCCD, this would not apply.

6. **Is reluctant to delegate tasks or to work with others unless they submit to exactly his or her way of doing things.**

In OCPD, this would be linked to the perfectionism. The

perfect world by perfect means. It would be more ego related.

In OCCD, this would be a part of the control. A perfect world be their standards. Not evident in the passive, but likely in the aggressive.

7. Adopts a miserly spending style toward both self and others; money is something to be hoarded for future catastrophes.

In OCPD, this would be symptomatic of the disorder. It should not be mistaken for someone who was brought up during the Great Depression, and subsequent generations who were taught to save at all costs.

In OCCD, this would be more obvious in the aggressive form. Money to support the habit would be tight, however, they would be inclined to show cash in front of others. It's part of the masking and feeds into the co-dependency. This would also be used as a measure of control, to give those close only what they need to do what they are expected to do.

8. Shows rigidity and stubbornness.

In OCPD, it would be a person with a firm belief that they are 100% right, and should not yield a position for any reason, unless they would allow themselves to be intentionally wrong.

In OCCD, this would be a last resort of maintaining control over others. In their minds, yielding would result in a loss of control, putting their world in a sort of chaos. It could also be a sign of weakness not to present rigidity.

Other Disorders

There are other Personality Disorders that might bear some similarities to OCCD, however, there is only rare or extreme similarities, not worth the comparison. Some would have more relevance in extreme circumstances. Personalities can change drastically when life circumstances change.

I have not covered any Anxiety Disorders, and for a good reason. These disorders would be prevalent as we discuss the psyche under the influence. I will break it down in the actual diagnosis section.

As you can see from the previous, it is easy to write off a person's behavior on an established disorder. Dishonesty is one trait a person with an addiction or alcoholism would have. They would not likely admit to another person as it being a factor in their thoughts or actions. It would be more common to blame it on others or a difficult life situation.

In another section I will be discussing behavior both in passive and aggressive. It is also important to know that the behavior can be a direct or indirect result of using an enabler. An enabler is a person who willingly or unwillingly helps a person function within this disorder.

This is usually done without that person knowing they are being used. Like a great magician, they keep your focus on something other than what they are trying to do. There are many reasons for why a person will be used and an enabler. I will also cover that later.

CHAPTER 4

OCCD Explained

Obsessive Compulsive Control Disorder

SIMPLE DEFINITION:

Obsessive Compulsive Control Disorder is an obsessive-compulsive disorder that uses control as the primary or principal motivation. It is at the base of Drug Addition, Alcoholism, and other abnormal behaviors.

A. Obsessions are defined by (1) and (2):
1. Persistent and recurrent thoughts, urges, and images that are experienced, about past deeds or regrets, at some time during the disturbance, as intrusive and unwanted, and that in most individuals cause marked anxiety or stress.
2. The individual attempts to suppress such thoughts, urges, or images, or to neutralize them with some other memory or action (i.e., performing a compulsion).

B. Compulsions are defined by (3) and (4):
   3. Repetitive behaviors (e.g., restless movements, check-
      ing, controlling people, places, or things) or mental acts
      e.g., counting, repeating words silently, showing little to
      no emotion) that the individual feels driven to perform
      in response to an obsession or according to rules that
      are rigidly applied.
   4. The behavior or mental acts are aimed at preventing
      or reducing anxiety or distress, or preventing some
      dreaded action or situation from the past; however,
      these behaviors or mental acts are not connected in a
      realistic way with what they are designed to neutralize
      or prevent, or are clearly excessive.

C. The obsessions or compulsions are time-consuming (e.g.,
   take more than one hour per day) or cause clinically significant distress or impairment in social, occupational, or
   other important areas of functioning.
   5. The obsessive-compulsive symptoms are not ex-
      clusively attributable to the physiological effects of a
      substance (e.g., alcohol, a drug of abuse) or another
      medical condition.
   6. Takes control of people, places, and things, in real or
      figurative terms, taking all rights, privileges, and respon-
      sibilities of total ownership.

There are two primary phases to this disorder, the Passive
Phase and the Aggressive Phase. There is also a transitional
phase we will call a Crossover Phase. In the Crossover phase,
a person can exhibit both Passive and Aggressive traits. It is
also common for the intensity of the Aggressive Phase to increase and decrease.

OCCD Passive Phase:

A person showing four or more of the following:

1. Rapid changes in expressions, more prevalent in groups, to find acceptance.
2. Considers relationships more passionate than they really are.
3. Looking for acceptance, but pulls away from groups giving acceptance, unless there is a measure of control given.
4. Shows a reluctance to share personal information, not based on shyness.
5. Unwilling to get involved with someone unless certain they will be liked.
6. Can become easily preoccupied with someone they feel to be a theat.
7. Feels inadequate in social situations.
8. Keeps negative comments from others while dismissing the positive comments.
9. Has difficulty trying new things for fear of failure, can't see the positive in trying.
10. Has anxiety when feeling abandoned, real or perceived.
11. Creates new self-image in attempt to please others.
12. Chronic feelings of emptiness or disappointment.
13. Restrained in relationships for fear of ridicule and disappointment.
14. Patterns of extreme idealization or devaluation within a relationship.

OCCD Aggressive Phase:

A person showing five or more of the following:

1. Uncomfortable with a person or group unless given desired attention.
2. Sexual desires and expressed deliberately.
3. Speaks in a theatrical tone (louder) to gain attention. Is to be hoarded, unless to impress others
4. Impulsively engage in self-destructive activities.
5. Pre-occupied with rules and details.
6. Is a perfectionist to their own standards and ideals.
7. Devoted to work and productivity.
8. Sees the world in black and white (absolute) terms.
9. Labels and categorizes people and doesn't allow for them to change.
10. Reluctant to delegate tasks unless assured they will be done their way.
11. Money is to be hoarded unless to impress others.
12. Becomes stubborn, ridged, aggressive, if their ideas are not accepted.
13. Plan big and enjoy the benefits of a project in their mind before they actually start it.
14. They get others to do their work and then take credit for indirect efforts.
15. Spend at least an hour a day reflecting on the past to put a better spin on it.
16. Become obnoxious when under the influence.
17. They require both attention and also a desired response.
18. Uses others by knowing their hot buttons and when to push them.
19. Thinks others are envious or jealous of them.

20. Sees themselves as the most important person in the lives of others.

THE PROTOTYPICAL CASE

Starting at birth, one or both parents are substance abusers, or grew up in a substance abusive home. From an early age, attention will be inconsistent, as in "Feast or Famine". They will get more than they can accept, or be left alone for long periods of time.

As they grow up from the toddler stage, they will understand winning is the only option and failure is unacceptable. This ideology is different than a successful person's ideology. With successful people, failure is not good, but it is learned from and some miscalculations are understood to be a part of the process. In a OCCD home, success and failure are a reflection of their self-worth. Success must come with an element of control, and failure comes with feeling disgraced. It is also taught they must please the Controller. From grades to extra-curricular activities, they strive to please and some adapt a "People Pleaser" mentality, while others will give up and become angry and envious.

As they hit the adolescent years, usually between 11 to 16, they will be feeling highly insecure about themselves and when drugs or alcohol is offered for an easy way to "Fit in", most will accept. It's at this time the substance works like gasoline on an open flame, and the psychological attachment is formed. The drug of choice will greatly enhance the ego, thus making the user feel in control, and not being controlled. This, along with the euphoric feeling creates a willingness to want it again.

The recovery, or sobering up period will turn them away from wanting to do it on their own, but with some encouragement, they do it again, and the habit is created. As their intellect grows, their maturity growth is stunted, thus leaving them with the five basic emotions of a toddler: crying sad, temper-tantrum, pouting, giddy happy, and paranoid. There are some adolescents who "Give up" fitting in and engage in risky or dangerous behavior. Some will over-eat, using food as a feel-good source.

For those who engage in substance use, they will find their peer will challenge them to do more at one time, much like a contest. It's here when the foundation is set in stone and the addiction is formed. For those who don't use, they find themselves will low self-esteem, high anxiety, and some level of depression. They have a low self-image and user or not, end up to be people pleasers, starting with the dominator in the family unit at an earlier age and growing to others they see they need in life. This is also how they learn to manipulate others to gain control over them.

When they reach young adulthood, they begin to notice that not everyone is doing what they are doing, or in the amounts they are using, and some see them as having a problem. They will gravitate to those who also have addictions in an effort to seem normal to themselves. Here is where they try to live in two realities, as people begin to walk away from them, they will desperately try to have a life with them, while still having a life where they can use and have those people supporting them so as not to feel they have a problem. This is where you can also see some levels of codependency.

The longer they go, the greater the gap between these two realities. They will concede to themselves they have a problem, but will have no desire to address the problem, because of the loss of one of their realities. Relationships on a long-term level, with come from those who use with them, or have met them while they are using. These relationships quickly become unhealthy because of the need for control. Men will be described as controlling, and women described as clingy. With a greater use, the mood swings will become more noticeable as every emotion will increase in intensity, even more so when under the influence.

As their life goes on, they will be consumed by what and who they don't have in their life, along with what and who they lost from their life. They will show little to no appreciation for who and what they have in their life. They will go to great lengths to take the surprise out of like, making sure they know everything that can and will happen.

As you can see, addiction plays a major role in the intensification of this disorder. It is problematic, thus changing a person's life drastically, and not for the better. Need for treatment is based solely on the effect the problem has on a person's life. This person could function normally with this disorder, however once problems become life altering, treatment is required.

There are people who are normal drinkers and then again there are also alcoholics. The question is, what is a threshold? Just as a person enters into an intoxication, there is a stop measure in the brain which one reach will cause a person to feel the same effects as they would of motion sickness.

Lightheadedness, dizziness, and nauseousness are the most common symptoms. It's on the other side of this discomfort is you will find intoxication. You yourself may have been intoxicated before but that doesn't make you a problem alcoholic. Because there are different degrees of alcoholism there is mild, moderate, and severe. So clearly every person who drinks is not an alcoholic in need of treatment.

Many people will ask if the same distinction can be said for marijuana users? The answer is no. Marijuana users typically use it to become intoxicated. There is no moderate social use of that drug. People use it with the intent to reach a euphoric plateau. There is no holding him a marijuana cigarette just to be social. For years many people have called it a gateway drug. It's not so much that it is a gateway drug as it leads to more and more euphoric plateaus and that's where the gate is opened.

CHAPTER 5

Where Was It?

Now the question is where exactly did I find this is disorder? It was actually found within the first step of the Alcoholics Anonymous (AA) Twelve Steps. Take a very close look at the verbiage used in that first step you will see they use the word "unmanageable" instead of "uncontrollable". You will find nowhere in the AA doctrine do they use the word control. Give to, manage, care of, but never control because they knew that control was in the core of the problem.

*We admitted we were powerless over alcohol, that our life had become **unmanageable**.*

Each word in the 12 Steps of AA was reviewed by the first 100 alcoholics to complete the steps to make sure each word meant exactly what they wanted it to say. As you look at the First Step, it talks about being "powerless" over alcohol, not helpless. The very first edition said "We admitted we were licked.". The idea behind that first step to admit to a problem and honesty being the principal behind it.

What many people misunderstand about AA is that it is an enigma. AA owns no property. AA has no employees because all of its work is done by volunteers. AA whisks into meetings just as they begin and whisks out just as they end. The chairperson at these meetings is not in charge, they are AA's one and only representative and like AA, has no opinion outside AA during the meeting. AA is one of the most successful self-help groups in the world. Its twelve steps have been adopted by other self-help groups both with and without permission.

What makes that unusual is the twelve steps won't keep anyone sober, won't keep anyone clean, won't stop someone from over-eating, won't stop someone from gambling. The twelve steps are there to help someone close the unfinished issues in their past and to keep them from creating new issues, period. This clearly shows that many people with different destructive traits have the same psychological issue. Thus, the "issue" is a symptom, not the problem. In this case, the symptom can be problematic.

In the first step, you can find the recipe for a relapse. Exchange the word "life" with the word "alcohol".

*We admitted we were powerless over **life**, that our **alcohol** had become unmanageable.*

It's common to have a lot of thoughts about something you have given up. So, when drinking thoughts come up, it's easier to say no when life is manageable. When life gets complicated, that's when the thoughts become a plan, and the plan becomes an action.

The word powerless is also significant. A synonym would be helpless. They chose the word powerless to instill the thought that alcohol could not be managed. When you take the word power alone, it could mean strength, energy, influence, or authority. When you can admit that alcohol is stronger that you, it would also mean you are not managing your life, alcohol is. The American Psychiatric Association (APA) summarizes 12 Steps of AA as follows:

Alcoholics Anonymous as summarized by the American Psychological Association, the process involves the following:

*Admitting that one **cannot control** one's alcoholism, addiction or compulsion;

*Recognizing a higher power that can give strength;

*Examining past errors with the help of a sponsor (experienced member);

*Making amends for these errors;

*Learning to live a new life with a new code of behavior;

*Helping others who suffer from the same alcoholism, addictions or compulsions.

In order to denounce control, you must first have to acknowledge that it is possible. There is where the APA has missed the true driver of alcoholism/addiction. They believe that alcohol can be controlled so recovery from alcoholism should be a matter of choice and will. The alcohol or drug is actually a byproduct of a larger issue.

The first three steps in AA and the APA differ in the third step. In AA, you turn your will and life over to a higher power. With the APA, you start looking for a root cause to the problem. Unfortunately, they don't look for or see a control issue. They generally look for something in the past that causes the behavior or brings on the urge to use.

AA is used by APA to give additional help and a safe place for the alcoholic to be. Of course, it is also used heavily by the court system. I will be covering some of the use and abuse later in this book. There is a wealth of information within the twelve steps of AA. Here is a summation of what is within those steps and the value they have.

Step 1:

We admitted we were powerless over alcohol, that our lives had become unmanageable.

The AA Approach:

There are two problems that we are making an admission to. The first is that our best of intentions and capabilities fell short to allow us to use alcohol as we desired. The second problem is that our life had become something that we no longer had the ability to direct as we wanted it. To look at how your life has transpired and to see the problem that you have is alcohol. Using a Cause & Effect methodology, you can see how the use of alcohol caused problems in your life that you were unable to solve yourself. You come to this conclusion through being completely honest with yourself.

The Psychological Approach:

Admitting you have a problem is a key to any treatment. When you are suppressing it, hoping it will go away or solve itself, you cannot treat the problem quite so easily. YOU have to make that assessment! No one else can tell you anything you are not ready to believe.

The Wisdom of The Step:

You will notice they use the word Powerless. That word is a key because of the many forms of power that there are. Power is strength, energy, influence, and authority. Every alcoholic has used all these forms of power to not only control their drinking, but also to control their lives. As the step is written, you see that alcohol caused problems or, without the use of alcohol, our lives would be just fine. What happens if you flip these two parts around? What if it read: We admitted that our lives had become unmanageable, and that we were powerless over alcohol? The answer is we would have the formula for relapse. Every person who relapses does not do it because life is going too well. They relapse when they have a problem they cannot solve. When life becomes overwhelming, and they feel "powerless" within it, that's when they become powerless over alcohol, the thought of drinking it. The formula also is why some people leave AA. They foster the belief that as long as their lives are manageable, they won't be powerless over alcohol. This means they can resume drinking and it won't become a problem unless they run into a serious problem, and then drink. They now have the power over alcohol and can prove it by their lives lacking problems.

Step 2:

Came to believe that a Power greater than ourselves could restore us to sanity.

The AA Approach:

In the first step, we admitted to having problems beyond our ability to correct them. The principal behind this step is hope. We are hopeful that there is a solution to our problem. This solution would have to come from something or someone outside of us. The solution would bring a normalcy back to our lives.

The Psychological Approach:

After admitting to a problem, it is always encouraged to seek help. A greater power could come in the form of help to address the problem. Within a group of people with the same disorder, you would have the opportunity to learn how to cope with the problem.

The Wisdom of the Step:

It again describes power. This time the power is greater than your own. The power is not described as "Higher", but merely "Greater". This would indicate that the power source you are looking for is more tangible. You within a group, for example, would always be greater than you alone. Within the

AA reading How It Works, it describes people sharing their experience, strength, and hope with each other. Strength is a form of power. When you share strength with someone, they become more powerful. So when they share it with you, you then have the "Greater Power". Sharing experiences also brings power because knowledge is power. This step directly applies to a meeting the others who have your condition.

Step 3:

Made a decision to turn our will and our lives over to the care of God as we understood Him.

The AA Approach:

Many in AA will debate the term "God", and some will question the existence of God. Others will find exception with the spiritual belief and refer back to their upbringing. Depending on the make-up of the group you are in when this topic is brought up for discussion will depend what you hear. Ideally, the concept is to accept a Higher Power in your life and turn to that Higher Power when you need direction in your life. The choices that You made up to that point have led you to the problems you now have.

The Psychological Approach:

Belief is something greater than yourself has always been a part of good mental health. The third step in treatment however, would be to locate the source of the initial problem (alcohol). When you can resolve that issue, the motivation to drink will diminish.

The Wisdom of the Step:

"turn our will and lives over" is the most important part of the step. When you consider, that most of the people who first walk into an AA Meeting, have lost something, and are on a course to lose everything. When you consider what your life would be like with nothing in it, it changes your perspective as to what you DO have in your life. The end result would be Gratitude. The principal behind this step is Faith. Many see this as a faith in a Higher Power. The actual faith comes in getting everything you need back through the faith in a Higher Power. This step is the first one that directly attacks the Ego. Its mission is to disable the thinking that you will always keep what you have gotten and what you get is not always because of what you did or who you are.

Step 4:

Made a searching and fearless moral inventory of ourselves.

The AA Approach:

To make a list of all that lies within you. Many see the focus must be on all the bad or undesirable traits they have. They get the idea from reading the steps that follow and trying to out-think the program. Some refuse to do this step because it brings back too many negative thoughts, they had about themselves. They see it as a chance to see what was causing the failure in their lives. How alcohol affected them and made them exhibit the kind of behavior they did. The final conclusion they hope to draw at the end of this step is that alcohol made them selfish.

The Psychological Approach:

Self-examination is always a good thing. Before we can progress and grow in life, we once in a while have to look at ourselves and see what we have done to help ourselves and what we have done to hurt ourselves. When we can make a realization of those things, we can avoid the negative and do more of the positive.

The Wisdom of the Step:

It is important to look at both the positives as well as the negatives of who we are. You can't overlook that despite all the knocks and pings you took, you still have something left. The question is, what are you afraid of seeing in yourself? The principal of the step is Courage. It takes courage to admit to shortcomings. Within the AA program, facing fear is an ongoing topic for discussion. What greater fear could you have than facing the monster from within you? If you can face this fear, no fear will be greater in your life. You will have the power to change your life anyway you want provided, you are truly honest with yourself. What you will find as the end result of your negative traits is Self-centeredness. Selfishness is an act and self-centeredness would be a motive. It's why you developed and used these traits.

Step 5:

Admitted to God, to ourselves, and to another human being the exact nature of our wrongs.

The AA Approach:

In this step, you come to grips with what you have done with all of those negative traits you had. In admitting to your Higher Power, yourself, and to another person, you have vented. You can walk away with the sense you no longer carry that feeling of guilt. You might also find that person to whom you make these admissions to might have done some similar things. In the final analogy, what did alcohol cause you to do and what did you become as a result. The principal of this step is Integrity. The point of the step is to make these admissions as full as possible.

The Psychological Approach:

It basically works as a therapy session. You're telling someone what has been bothering you and in working with someone (a Sponsor), you can find some resolution to these issues and relieve some of the pain that is caused by guilt and concealment.

The Wisdom of the Step:

When you trace the path of a lie, it looks very similar to this step. First, you have to believe in the lie. Then, you ask your Higher Power to allow your lie to be believable, and then you ask another person to accept your lie as true and factual. Why is this path relevant? A person with an addiction will, at the very least, lie to themselves that they have a problem. Then they will ask their Higher Power to overlook their problem, and then lie to cover up their problem to others. Basically, if you can lie to yourself without remorse, you can lie to anyone. In the First Step, you started being honest with yourself. In AA, the motto "To thy own self be true" is on every sobriety coin. The message is to be truthful to yourself and others. The objective is to get back something you lost: Your Integrity. Integrity is the principal of this step.

Step 6:

Were entirely ready to have God remove all these defects of character.

The AA Approach:

If you take the list created from doing the Forth Step, you will see a number of things about yourself you don't like. Some of these are easily fixed, while others have been a part of your everyday living for years. Just as you asked your Higher Power to take away your desire to drink, you will also be asking your Higher Power to take away these defects of character. Remember as it says in The Promises of AA "God will do for me what I cannot do for myself."

The Psychological Approach:

This step does not really apply in psychological terms other than to understand that there might be a God, and you are not it.

The Wisdom of the Step:

As you learned in the Forth Step, the summation of your behavior was actually based on the motivation the blame away from yourself. Actually, some of the things you would call a "defect" can help you in treating your addiction. Procrastination and selfishness are two examples of such defects. You can procrastinate yielding to drinking and that would help keep you sober. You also need to be selfish about your sobriety, not putting it where you might lose it. The true character defect that you need to rid yourself of is self-centeredness. When it is mixed with alcohol, it becomes a dominant personality trait and a root cause for your social woes and mishaps.

Step 7:

Humbly asked Him to remove our shortcomings.

The AA Approach:

This step is an extension of Step 6. Once you have identified what you need to get rid of, it is now up to you to ask your Higher Power to help you. The principal behind this step is Humility. Asking your Higher Power, to do something for you, that will benefit you and those around you. To help you become a better person and the person you want to be.

The Psychological Approach:

It is always recommended to acknowledge something greater than yourself. To maintain a sense that your actions could have consequences promotes inhibitions. The belief in "Faith Healing" is not supported widely.

The Wisdom of the Step:

This is the first time within working the steps that you are actually starting a dialog with your Higher Power. You can start to foster the belief that your Higher Power doesn't just watch over you, but can have a direct impact on how you live your life and how your life will turn out. As you turned your will and your life over to your Higher Power in Step 3, you are now trying to remove the obstacles that would prevent that from happening. It also allows you to see the power of your Higher Power. You will gain the sense that you are not alone in your daily struggles and that help can be just a prayer away. Between Step 2 (Greater Power) and Step 7 (Higher Power), you can now see for yourself the power that you have to change your life for the better.

Step 8:

Made a list of all persons we had harmed, and became willing to make amends to them all.

The AA Approach:

This is an extension from Step 5, where you made your admissions to what regrettable things you did and whom you did them to. This step allows to get rid of some of those demons that have been haunting you. This step isn't quite that easy. First, you have to identify these people, and then see if it is possible. Some have died off and some have moved away. Others did things to you as well. Some people see this step as a way to rebuild broken relationships.

The Psychological Approach:

This is a way to overcome fear. It would make you more self-dependent and less co-dependent. Your setting a stage for hearing the worst about yourself and making that confrontation will help you grow and mature.

The Wisdom of the Step:

The key word in this step is "willing", the principal behind the step is Willingness. The step puts no claim on people from your past. You will have also seen by now that this program starts in the center (with you) and works its way outward. Your list should start with those who are still in your life. To make amends is also a key part of this step. Talk is cheap so saying you're sorry won't carry a whole lot of weight. Making things right by that person would go a lot farther. Would you have the willingness to go the extra mile?

Step 9:

Made direct amends to such people wherever possible, except when to do so would injure them or others.

The AA Approach:

As directly linked to Step 8, you now go forward into the World and find these people you have harmed and are making apologies and fixing the damage that you have caused. As you can start now to feel better about yourself, others might notice a change in you as well. You might find this can restart relationships that ended and might strengthen those you currently have. As the Big Book points out, it is about here you will see The Promises of AA coming true.

The Psychological Approach:

This is a way to overcome fear. It would make you more self-dependent and less co-dependent. Moving forward will give you a greater feeling of self-worth and independence.

The Wisdom of the Step:

The principal of this step is Justice. It is not designed to be easy and not created for rewards. Many who think this step is about rebuilding relationships could be very disappointed. YOU did something wrong to someone. YOU are now coming forward to make things right. These people didn't summon you to do this, you are doing it for your own reasons. The only "reward" that you could possibly ask for is forgiveness. That is not always related to restarting a relationship. You also have to keep in mind that some people have moved on. That some have forgotten you and some maybe thought of you as dead. You have to consider your appearing in their lives might cause harm to them, where they relive all those feelings of hurt. You asked your Higher Power to remove your self-centeredness. This would be a test of that. Clearly, Alcoholics and Addicts suck at apologies. If you combine steps four thru nine, you have the perfect apology.

Hello (fill in the blank)
I was a real Step 4,
Because of that I Step 5'd,
I Step 6 and Step 7'd,
Because you meant a lot to me (Step 8)
I am here to tell you I'm sorry and want to know at least how I can make it up to you (Step 9).

It is closure to those issues in the past that get in the way of them enjoying today. That is why Alcoholics Anonymous can make bold promises and know they will happen.

Step 10:

Continued to take personal inventory and when we were wrong promptly admitted it.

The AA Approach:

This is the first step in what are considered to be "Maintenance Steps". The objective is to keep your house in order and to address problems when they come up. It is common for an addicted person to avoid problems and hope they go away.

The Psychological Approach:

It falls in line with building healthy habits. We are all creatures of habit and this step promotes a healthier way of living and preventing a relapse.

The Wisdom of the Step:

You have now seen the benefits of sober living. You know what it took to get there. To think you did it all by yourself is foolish. To maintain gratitude and humility will help prevent the character defects from returning. It is also helpful to keep your mistakes small. We all make mistakes and for you to walk away from them would provide a breeding ground for lies and deception. You can "Keep It Simple" by admitting to mistakes when they happen. As you have found out, saying you are sorry carries far better when YOU spot the mistake than if you wait for someone to show it to you.

Step 11:

Sought through prayer and meditation to improve our conscious contact with God, as we understood Him, praying only for knowledge of His will for us and the power to carry that out.

The AA Approach:

It's where you start a relationship with the God of your understanding. You are not limited or obligated to any scripture. As it also says, you pray for what your God wants, not what you want. You will find in meetings that the discussion on this step will lead in many different areas. Some will discuss theology, some will talk about prayer, and some will lead the discussion into religion.

The Psychological Approach:

Again, modern psychology doesn't subscribe to faith healing. There is however something to be said for gathering your thoughts.

The Wisdom of the Step:

Prayer and Meditation, the prayers give a direct contact line to your Higher Power and meditation has a power of its own. Meditation has been used for centuries in Asia. Most notably, it is used in the martial arts. It is a way to bring your mind, body, and spirit together as one. You gain a three-prong attack with a single purpose. You truly learn how to master the power from within, while taking direction from a Higher

Power. Respecting your Higher Power is what gives pause to making bad choices. It's no longer just up to you, and you alone. Having something or someone else to answer to for your actions is an important part of supporting your choice not to drink.

Step 12:

Having had a spiritual awakening as the result of these Steps, we tried to carry this message to alcoholics, and to practice these principles in all our affairs.

The AA Approach:

This is where you show off what you have done to repair the damage you did to yourself. You will find most people commenting about "walking the talk". It is a step where you reach out to others who are like you were and help them find what you have.

The Psychological Approach:

Helping others is a health activity. When a person can see outside themselves, and help those who need it, it fosters positive social traits. It also shows a maturity in social interaction.

The Wisdom of the Step:

In the early days of AA, no one was ordered to attend meetings. A person saw their lives slipping away and wanted to stop the damage. This is how timeless AA is. Without changing a word in the Step, it still applies to what it originally meant.

With Court Systems ordering people to attend AA, most people not only have heard about AA, but have an opinion of it. To find people who need what AA offers and are willing to go to AA is slim. The timelessness is in how you use this Step. Considering that people are ordered into AA, how you speak of it during the meeting is now how to work this Step. You have an opportunity to say what AA has done for you. Not just in a person's first meeting, but in all the meetings you are in. This Step has always been about sponsorship. When you have worked through the Steps, you would then be qualified to help someone else. You can do this one-on-one or as a member of a group. Many times, it is a collective effort by several members to clearly explain a topic or help someone with a problem. You actually work the Step by showing up to meetings regularly and contributing to the discussion.

CHAPTER 6

The Overuse and Abuse of AA

The year was 1940, and the place was a courtroom in Akron, OH. It was there where the Fellowship of AA addressed the court, pleading to release the drunken inmates to them. They had a way to treat them that would stop them from drinking. They said these people suffered from Alcoholism, and said it was a psychological disorder. They had created a twelve-step program that would help these poor souls rebuild their lives. The Judge, who was probably tired of dealing with these poor souls, agreed to release them for treatment with this group called Alcoholics Anonymous.

With the success of the Akron, OH, group, came other groups and soon the practice was used nationwide. The difference was there were no members of the fellowship in these courtrooms. The inmates were released and told to attend AA meetings without notice being given to the fellowship. These people were given slips to be filled out by the fellowship members to show they had attended. These slips were not discussed in that courtroom in Akron, OH.

Date	Time	Place	Topic	Chairperson

In my research, I attended several meetings not just to observe, but also to participate. Many college professors send their psychology students to these meetings to observe them. Some groups allow this, so long as they know what these people are there for and no one in the group objects. One problem is some students won't identify themselves and some college professors think the AA groups are public domain, free for anyone to observe. That is not the case.

The part that really makes this fellowship work is anonymity. The fact no one outside of these groups know who they are. In some cases, it can jeopardize someone's career or business. There is also a privacy credo that "What is said should not pass into the outside world.". This gives the participants a sense of confidentiality and encourages openness in sharing.

As you can see by the example slip, someone must give their name to validate the slip. Some slips also request a phone number. What is being discussed must also be stated. These groups are not funded in any way, shape, or form by any court or state agency. Yet by their intrusiveness, you would think they were.

Additionally, the probationers/parolees are "sent" to AA meetings. There is no one from the fellowship to welcome them or agree to sponsor or mentor them. They are simply sent out to find "a meeting". There is a gross over expectation that someone will do the work for the criminal justice community and not only watch over these people, but also teach them about addiction/alcoholism as it relates to them.

This makes the AA a de-facto probation office and the members of the fellowship de-facto probation personnel. The primary purpose of these meetings is "to stay sober and help other alcoholics achieve sobriety". How can this be accomplished when the premise of these people is to comply to and finish their time? They don't walk in with the idea of staying clean and sober. Most are playing the game to get out of trouble and to go back to their old life, as it was.

These slips are not just used by the criminal justice departments, they are also use by the licensing departments to decide if someone can get their driving privileges restored. All of the AA fellowship names find their way into those files also. They even go so far as to quiz the petitioners on the meanings of the doctrine of AA. Clearly these departments have no right to use anything related to AA or its fellowship, but they do it anyway because they are the Government, and AA is an enigma.

So now we have judges handing out what amounts to a search

warrant to its probationers/parolees, to execute a search of the fellowship of AA. Why is this happening? You would have to go to the state legislature. They are after quick, easy, and cheap ways to address drunk driving and also empty their jails and prisons. They are the ones behind the abuse because they write the laws and legal procedure for those convicted (or plead guilty) of crimes. In my research, I have found most of all crimes are committed by someone under the influence of drugs or alcohol, or because of drugs or alcohol. There is a great need for some programs, but not at the expense of the public.

These legislatures must understand that their sending people to AA must be voluntary. According to Smartrecovery.org, the 9th US Court of Appeals made that ruling in the case of Hazle V. Crofoot, 727 F.3rd 983, in February, 2007. The case was about Hazle being ordered to attend AA by Crofoot, and that order violated Hazle's rights under religious freedoms.

AA was never designed to get people sober or keep people sober. It was designed to help people stay sober and repair the damage in their lives caused by drinking. The meetings are for helping people get through challenging parts of their lives without drinking. It amazed me how many people sent by the courts misunderstood this concept. Some think it's talk therapy, and others think it's a practice for what they will tell the court officer. Others will use it to get someone from the fellowship to write a letter of recommendation so they can get their driver's license back.

Even with all this turmoil, according to **mericanaddiction-centers.org**, AA's success rate is between 8% to 12%. A study conducted in 2014 concluded this and among approximately 6000 participants:

27% were sober less than one year
24% were sober 1 to 5 years
13% were sober 5 to 10 years
14% were sober 10 to 20 years
22% were sober over 20 years

The commitments I have seen the courts hand down are usually at least two years. If it's a Felony case, that commitment can be up to five years.

Oddly enough, the twelve steps seem to be the hot ticket item. At the time of this book, only two other organizations have permission to use the twelve steps, the sister group Ala-Non, and Narcotics Anonymous (NA). All the other groups that use them do it without permission, largely because AA is an enigma. Sad to know they didn't even ask.

I met several people who belong to more than one group. Some were AA and Ala-Non, and some were AA and NA. I also met people who were convicted of a drug crime who were ordered to go to AA. There are some people who are cross-addicted, but not all of those who I met were cross-addicted.

Once again, this would be the court's abuse of the AA fellowship. There is a sizeable difference between alcoholism and addiction. No one ever became an addict because they were just being sociable. If someone uses marijuana or drugs, it is to get buzzed, high, or stoned. People can become alcoholics by simply holding a drink to look sociable.

Of all the topics I have heard in my research, there is one that hardly ever comes up. I brought it up once and the room went eerily silent. That topic was "Blackouts". It is where the person goes into a concussion like state. They act and react like anyone else, but the next day, they have no recollection of what they did or where they were at.

A blackout is like a concussion in that a path in the brain is burned after the first one and the second one comes more quickly than the first. The third one more easily than the second and so on. The big question is how does a person act and react without knowing that they are? The brain reverts to the first time the person was drunk. So, for example; if the person was fifteen and rebellious, that is how they will act when they are blacked out.

CHAPTER 7

Other Disorders Associated With OCCD

Domestic Violence

Domestic violence would be the last resort available to someone who was attempting to control another person. Someone who commits domestic violence doesn't start out being violent, as a general rule. It is usually the last resort available. There are some who are violent by nature, but most are not.

The violence can also start when the conflict becomes personal. When someone's ego or sense of self are felt to be in question. A person will not generally act out when attacked on their ego. People are very secure in who they are and what their shortcomings are. It's when the alter ego is attacked, and again, that's the part on the psyche that is who we think we should be or who we want recognition for being.

When the conflict gets to that point, there is something else at stake. There is time and effort invested. There is also a desire not to have the conflict again. So, there would also be a goal not to just win, but to see the other person lose. When they would submit to their will.

Of course, when the violence has ended, that person will apologize and promise never to do it again. The problem is human nature tells us it will happen again. Everything is easier and is done better a second time we do something. The fact it was successful will add to that belief. As you saw in the addict/alcoholic apologies, the "I'm sorry" without any follow up to why they did it and what they are doing to insure it will never happen again are absent.

The controlling in a relationship may not always be violent, it can also be psychological. Many of those who resort to violence try the use of psychological manipulation. This can be as or even more devastating than a physical altercation. In a physical altercation, you can cover up to protect yourself. You can also look for a chance to strike one blow that will stop the attack. In a psychological attack, it usually is targeted on a weak point, something someone might be self-conscious about. This gives the attacker a distinct advantage as the victim would have no way to cover up and is generally too hurt or too stunned to make a counter-attack.

It is generally about dominance. One person trying to impose their will upon another and have that person live in a controlled environment. To make someone not have another opinion than what they are given. To stay in a psychological box where the controller wants them and not to venture out.

To remain the same, to not experience growth and development that all people need. In order to do this, they need to have or develop in someone certain traits. Let us explore those traits and tendencies.

Domestic Victims:

They become unwilling to show things about themselves. This would be a result of heavy and pointed criticism from someone they trusted not to hurt them. Notice that I did not say life partner. This person can also be a parent. You don't have to be in a partner relationship to suffer abuse. Child abuse can be referred to differently, but the abuser uses the same techniques and has the same psychological disorder.

They feel restrained in relationships. They don't feel free to be themselves, rather they try to be someone whom everyone expects them to be. Some people might use the phrase "people pleaser". This would not apply because a pleaser would make it a short time effort. This would be something long term and involve personality changes that would be noticeable to those who know them best.

They tend to be pre-occupied with criticism. We all try to better ourselves, and one way for that to happen is when someone gives us feedback. This would be something that effects how they feel about themselves. Their self-worth would be damaged. As a result, they would fear rejection in social situations. They would be more likely to act upon co-dependency, to act more overtly like a pleaser.

Self esteem would also be diminished. They would see

themselves as socially inept, inferior, and unappealing. They would be more likely to live within the view of the abuser. They would try harder to live up to their expectations of them and less about what they would like to be themselves. The feeling of being trapped within a relationship, with no escape possible.

They can make overt efforts to be pleasers. When an opportunity arises, they will be one of the first to volunteer to help. They will look for approval from others to build some self-esteem. The co-dependency will again be triggered and they will look for the affirmation in others they don't see of feel from themselves.

Damage from a controlling relationship is also a diminished sense of self. They don't see in themselves as the rest of the World sees them. They feel unworthy and inadequate. They don't identify themselves with any group or cause. They lose track of things and people they once enjoyed.

A side effect of an abusive relationship is an under developed Alter Ego. They have no desire to live beyond who and what they are. We need our Alter Ego to expand our horizons and to grow as a person. Without it, we will become dull and boring to others and uninterested in new and different things.

There are also chronic feelings of emptiness. Not exactly depression, but a sense of loss and some detachment. Feelings of boredom with various things without ever trying them. The feeling that life has passed you by and there is nothing to show for it.

Bullying

When we think about bullying, we typically think of a kid on a playground calling names, or pushing and shoving another kid. No one wants their child to be bullied, but it does exist. There are other kinds of bullies in our society. They exist in boardrooms and bars. It can be intoxicating to a person to impose their will on another person, to control them in what they think and how they feel about themselves. That is why the bullying doesn't stop after they finish school.

As the bully gets older, they learn to use other methods. They will sometimes have an agenda. Other times, they may just look to feed their Alter Ego. As they get more experience, they might try to bully more people or just those who can advance their wants and desires.

One way is to get others to do the work. Then if there is praise to be gained, they step forward and give the impression they did it single handedly. However, if there is fault with it, they are quick to blame others. At times they will even state how they told others the correct way, and they wouldn't listen.

Failure and blame are two things that bullies are not equipped to accept. They seldom had setbacks growing up and didn't accept blame because they could bully someone into not saying they were involved. They don't handle rejection well because they never grew as a person in their younger years.

Bullies live largely in their Alter Egos. These Alter Egos need to be fed regularly. To that extent, they require attention on a regular basis. Many times, they will act out to get the attention they are after. Other times they will find someone weaker and impose their will on them. This is a performance to them and it gets attention. They tend to get uncomfortable if the attention is paid to them when they want it. This is generally when their cruel streak comes out.

A bully will commonly use others. The question is if a person has been used, why would they allow themselves to be used again? The answer is in the person's hot buttons. Bullies are very good at finding hot buttons. When they were kids, they would find something that another kid was deathly afraid of or really didn't want to do, and then make them choose what they would face. Bullies remember these hot buttons and will use them as long as they are effective. This is the power they use to control others.

They are quite impulsive when it comes to something that get them attention or otherwise feeds their Alter Ego. It can be an activity or just an opportunity to showcase themselves. They see others as playthings and will use them like props on a stage. They love to entertain and see themselves as a huge star.

When it comes to others, they have relationships with, they keep them in "boxes". The term boxes refer to a place in life where a person is confined to who they are and where they are. It doesn't allow for any personal growth or development. They feel threatened when a person tries to leave their box. It generally is when they are most likely to become cruel and possibly violent.

Teen Suicide

When we talk about a controlling person, we tend to forget about the victims and how adversely they might be affected and to what degree. Of course, there is depression associated with it. The driver of it is not only sadness, but also the fact there are likely more than one controlling person they have a relationship with. One controller can certainly be within the family unit, but the second can be within a social unit, with the potential of a third being within a professional unit.

Whereas the AA fellowship uses the word powerless, the teen contemplating suicide would more likely use the word helpless. They would likely see the World as an unkind place where their thoughts and feelings are not welcome. Where they exist to please others, but not themselves. They see no means of escape and see life as it is as never-ending helplessness.

They tend to close themselves off to others. Not completely, but they keep private their innermost self. They are embarrassed by their circumstances and don't want anyone to see what is happening to them. They have close relationships, but those would be limited by time and space. There will always be things that are never divulged, no matter how intimate or long a relationship is.

Thus, they tend to keep more superficial relationships. Nothing too close or time consuming. They will be likely collecting friends to show normalcy. They will even date just to keep appearances. It is how they hide their pain so others won't suspect or ask.

Despite these relationships, they view themselves very harshly. They find faults where there are none such as ineptness in some social situations. They see themselves as inferior to others and tend to be very critical about their appearance. This can be fueled by controllers in their lives, or the fact they are trying to please a controller and their efforts are rejected.

They are not codependent, but do rely on the approval of others in their attempts to be a pleaser. There are certain expectations controllers will put on them and they will look to others to see if they are making progress. When a controller is near, they may seem nervous or jittery.

They also may have difficulty expressing some emotions. Empathy could be one of those. With having difficulty expressing their inner feelings, they may have trouble understanding what others are feeling from time to time. They might also experience periods of emptiness, where they don't have feelings of their own, where they would be unable to relate to others.

Detecting a teen at risk is only a part of it. The biggest part is finding what is happening and how to correct it. You would be dealing with at least two persons whom likely wouldn't want to relinquish control. Within the family unit is certainly the hardest to deal with. There would be a good chance the person has been doing this for a long time and won't give it up because they feel it is normal, natural, and it works.

Cell Phone Addiction

Can cell phone use really be an addiction? I know many ask the question and wonder what the thresholds are for addiction. A broad-brush explanation would be a physiological attachment to a substance or object that would create an adverse reaction if taken away, as in a withdrawal. The simple explanation would be does it create problems in a person's everyday life and could these problems make them a danger to themselves and others. The answer explanations would be yes. So, what makes it a problem?

A person becomes pre-occupied with details in their life and the lives of others. This becomes even more problematic when a person is willing to discard facts that are not in favor or flattering to their position. Without facts, we have nothing to base our plans or experiences on. We need to know what we have and don't have to make decisions. Without all the facts, our lives would them become very complicated.

People who engage in this behavior are generally perfectionists. They are looking for perfection in themselves, their life, and the person and lives of those who are close to them. Clearly, the Cell Phone then becomes a tool in the control of others. Think about the kinds of texts you get. Where are you? Who are you with? What are you doing? What are you thinking? Do you miss me? Etc.

These people are also paranoid of unexpected change. Change is already difficult, but when the person has no time to prepare for it, and likely no input in it, it creates a huge problem. Their World depends on knowing where everyone is and what everyone is doing. When that is altered in even a small way, their peace of mind is shattered and they go into crisis mode.

They also many times see things in absolutes, in black or white, without any shades of grey. They may not speak in stereo types by terms, but will use stereo types to define a person, place, or thing. These stereo types are not limited to race, creed, national origin, sex, or religion. Political stereo types as of 2020 seem to be very socially acceptable. They have not only been used by political figures, but also members of the media. They will also speak in extremes to make their statement seem more convincing.

There is also a tendency to become stubborn or ridged. This usually happens when their control is threatened. If someone takes too long to respond, or if they are not giving all the information requested. Also, if someone is sharing time while they are texting with them. This might lead to frantic efforts to gain full attention. Sometimes the reason for this is to avoid abandonment or the feeling of being left out of it.

Generally, a person will feel uncomfortable unless given proper attention. This would mean getting all the information they request and to have the feeling the other person needs them and will always need them. The other person will not only ask for their advice, they will use it.

In many ways, these relationships are perceived to be greater than they really are. The passion one person feels may not be equal to what the other person feels. This also creates conflict by limiting the time the other person would give to the exchange. Thus, the feelings of self-importance will take a hit and leave a person depressed. It can be a shock to find out you are not quite as important as you thought you were.

Given the time devoted to these devices, and the urgency people put on the responses to them, it would be easy to see why Cell Phones are an addiction. The time you spend on them at work can get you fired. Thus, creating problems and complications in your life. Using them while you drive creates a risk to yourself and other drivers. Clearly Cell phone use can be used to control others by gathering information on other people, knowing what is going on in their life, knowing what they are thinking, and directing what they will do next, also qualifies in the addiction category.

CHAPTER 8

Enablers

Enabler is a term that describes a person who helps an addict/ alcoholic to live in both the World they are in and the World they want to be in. An Enabler is not limited to only those persons, they can also help a Domestic Abuser or Bully. Again, there is the World they are in and the one they want to be in. They themselves will not be the same person in both Worlds. As we have learned, there is both an Ego and Alter Ego in play. We will refer to this person as an Abuser.

Many times, an Enabler is a family member. Sometimes a parent, brother, or sister, other times a spouse, and sometimes a child. There are also no limits to the number of Enablers a person is using. It sounds complicated so I'll use an example of someone I knew.

This man was a 24/7 alcoholic. He always had alcohol in his system. I met him in a bar (of all places), and he was the life of the party type. He was very friendly, in some ways a little too friendly. I became his friend, and unknowingly, one of his Enablers.

He had several Enablers. To know him was to be one of his minions in one way, shape or form. His main Enabler was his sister. She would stop by to visit him and would be concerned about his health. She knew he drank a lot, but never could associate his health concerns with the amount he drank or the frequency that he drank.

Eventually he lost his job because of his drinking. He had worked for the same company for over 30 years. They took their time building a case for termination, even had a private detective watch him after they ordered him to rehab as a condition of future employment. After he was terminated, he met with his daughter and his sister and they discussed sending him into rehab on their own. If he had gone when the company ordered him to, the company could have gotten updates on his progress and that was his excuse to not go. He told his sister if he went, they would spread around the shop what he was saying and doing to his treatment.

The last time I spoke to his was that night. He told me he was really going to rehab and he talked it all over with his daughter and sister. He said he didn't care how long it took; he wouldn't leave until they said he was ready. It's a funny thing about drunks, they don't know it but they think out loud when they are drunk. It was during that call he told me he was going to sign in and then sign out. He would have to stay three days but then he could come home and hang out on his couch for two weeks to "get himself straight". While he was doing that, his sister would talk to the company and get his job back.

His sister never did get his job back, but her duties as an Enabler were not over. His health steadily declined and his sister was there to give some other medical reasons for his poor health. She thought he had ALS, Lou Gehrig disease, and wanted him to get tested. Of course, this was what he told other people he met, that he actually has ALS and needed to get more testing done. He died in a house fire. He was using an old toaster oven and the current draw overloaded wiring causing the insulation to burn. The house was around 100 years old so that was old insulation and he was likely passed out on the couch when it started. No one else was hurt in that fire.

Within this example, you can see some character traits. Abusers who use Enablers will plan big. Nothing is too big or too grand. They themselves will not be doing any of the work from this plan, that is where others come in. They will sit back and direct and have others do the actual work. As in the example, the sister would get his job back, not him. The sister would explain why he wouldn't go to rehab when the company ordered him to go, not him.

With everyone else doing their work for them, you would think an Abuser is lazy. No that's not it. There is a reason they get others to do the work, and that reason is so there is always someone else to blame if things go badly. Also, some-things would be unpleasant to discuss and would harm their Alter Ego. A lot of strategy goes into picking who they will use and how that person will be used. When things go well, the Abuser is ready to tale full credit. After all, it was their plan and their recruitment of talent.

The terms Should of, Would of, and Could of, make up a sig-nificant part of their dialog when speaking of the past. There is also always someone else to blame when things went wrong. There is also likely a reference to how they were victimized. As you can see, there is a trend to avoid taking blame. Admitting failure would seriously damage their Ego or Alter Ego.

A quick and basic make up of an Abuser is they have the intellect of an adult, and the emotional maturity of a toddler. This sounds odd but consider their development. Did they ever have to manage their life? Did they ever have to restrain their emotions? Mostly with Addicts/Alcoholics, they did develop some emotional maturity, but under the influence, they revert back to a toddler. A toddler has 5 basic emotions; giddy happy, crying their eyes out sad, temper tantrums, pouting, and paranoia. Under the influence, Addict/Alcoholics display the same basic emotions and like a toddler, they don't have any way to moderate it, it's either full blast or not at all, and there is no way to blend those emotions either. Some people call them mood swings, but they are really just an Addict/Alcoholic, changing moods.

The Abuser is very first person orientated. The World starts with them and ends with them, with plenty of them in between. So, it seems logical that they would over exaggerate their problems. They also see themselves as critically important to everything in the center of a conversation. The Abuser is not however feeding their Ego, but instead, their Alter Ego.

They become co-dependent when it comes to their Alter Ego. After all, that is what they want the World to see and to identify them as. They look for validation, first from the enablers and then from others who may be around. They can also go through bouts of depression when they fail to live up to who they are in the Alter Ego. This can also have an effect on who they are in the real World.

The Enabler is the person who helps create the illusion that the Abuser is living in two Worlds at the same time. They feed the Alter Ego as the Abuser would have them do it. Abusers can be very crafty and deceptive. There might be times an Enabler doesn't realize they are being used. Again, it all fits in to the Abuser knowing what buttons to push and when.

Part of the deception is for the Enabler not to see or realize how bad the Abuser really is. It could be a Domestic Abuser convincing the Enabler that every relationship is like theirs's is, or an Addict/Alcoholic getting the Enabler to believe that their problem is not really that bad, they just see them when they are going through some rough times. The Abuser will always have excuses for their behavior, but never a plan of solution, of how they can get past their problems and get back into normal living.

The Abuser will insist the problems they have are temporary, and that there is no need to worry about it. The real problem is that there will always be a "temporary problem" as long as they have an Enabler to use. They work on sympathy and em-pathy from the Enabler. Unfortunately, they themselves don't have the capacity to have either one.

The Enabler is helping to feed the main core problem, and likely doesn't know it. They are given stories where the Abuser is a poor victim and has no one else to help them. They will likely try to get the Enabler to volunteer to help, but if all else fails, they will ask them to help. Either way, once you start helping, you are in for the long haul. Every time they need something you can do for them, they will ask, or give another story of how no one will help them after all they have done for them.

At first, the helping doesn't seem so bad. The tasks are pretty simple and well within your comfort range. As time goes on, these tasks won't be so simple, or they won't be something you can quickly do and be back to your life. The appreciation is there at the beginning also. As time goes on, that too will disappear and you will have regular assignments. There will also be an expectation placed on the Enabler to do these tasks because they have always done them before.

At this point, an Enabler begins to feel used. Their self esteem begins to erode. If they try telling the Abuser they won't do it anymore, the Abuser uses the ties they have to bind them to continue. It might be questioning a loyalty as a friend, or holding family honor over their head. There is always something they can use and that makes the Enabler feel trapped and powerless to change the situation.

The Abuser will continue to use the leverage they have. While doing that, they also see they might have a revolt on their hands. They will try to comfort the Enabler into a routine and tell them how refusal is actually hatred. That adds a new wrinkle to their leverage, now questioning a person's empathy and generous nature. While still using whatever relationship bonds that are available. There is also the opposite approach, where they will complement the Enabler for all they have done and say what a truly good person they are. This all depends on the person, their hot buttons, and their situation. In a violent relationship, the Abuser will actually try to convince their victim that they are also to blame and that things wouldn't have gotten out of hand if they had done as they were expected.

There is also an emotional rollercoaster that takes place. These are mood swings because they are from manufactured crisis by the Abuser. Mostly to get attention and sympathy. Over time, these will seem routine and almost predictable. Another reason for these episodes is to get the Enabler to not believe what they see or what others might be telling them. By this point, the Enabler is usually hooked in and always to some degree, will be used by the Abuser.

CHAPTER 9

Social Impact of OCCD

We will start with the following example;

Johnny has a bag of apples. These are not special apples, but Johnny happens to collect them. Johnny meets Mary. Mary bakes pies, and her specialty is apple pies. As Johnny and Mary talk, they are getting to know each other and that is when Johnny gives his bag of apples to Mary. Mary is happy to accept the apples and then Johnny goes on his way.

Mary now has to make a choice as to what to do with these apples. She can bake them in a pie, she can throw them away, or she gave give them to someone else. She has to make a choice soon because the apples won't keep forever. So, Mary decides to bake them in pies.

As the law is, Johnny has no responsibility for the apples or the pies. He doesn't have to buy packaging for them or pay for the delivery of these pies to whomever Mary sells them to. If Mary threw them away, he would have no obligation to pay for disposal fees, and would not have to be consulted to whom Mary would have given the apples to.

Mary does not have to share the pies with Johnny because he gave the apples to Mary of his own free will. Mary, for the same reason, does not have to share any profits of the pie sales with Johnny. Mary does not need Johnny's permission to discard the apples, nor to give them away.

Johnny has no legal right to the apples because he gave them to Mary, of his own free will, with no conditions set in place before the transfer. Johnny has no responsibility for what Mary does with those apples because she had full rights and with full rights comes full responsibility. She assumed them when she accepted the apples.

In this example, it is pretty easy to see what's right and wrong. It seems strange I would tell a story like this in a book about a psychological disorder. Now if we, for example, change "baking pies" to pregnancy, and "apples" into man byproduct, or fetus, this takes on a whole new meaning and the simplicity that it once had is gone.

This book is being written in the year 2020, so things may change after its release. Abortion has been legal in the United States since January, 1973, after the Supreme Court ruled on the case Roe V Wade. One of the over looked parts of that ruling was the high court unanimously (9-0) ruled that sexual privacy was a Constitutional right. This plays into the woman having the total and unquestioned right to end a pregnancy.

Nearly every law on the books in the United States is

predicated on the concept that when you make a decision, you own the outcome. If, for example; you pull out a gun, and it goes off and kills someone, you can be charged with at least negligent homicide or manslaughter, because you made the decision to pull out the gun. Without that act, it could be argued the person would not have been shot. The same could be said for a drunk driving fatality. Your decision to get drunk, your decision to drive, your responsibility for what happens as a result.

Since this has been the law of the land for almost 50 years, people have always been passionate about it on both sides, some for, and others against. If fact, most people allow all of their political beliefs to rest solely with one of two parties. If you are in favor of abortion, you probably believe in gun control, and if you are against abortion, you are probably against gun control.

For almost 50 years, the two parties have led the United States electorate around by the nose. Going from the example, there are some questions to be asked. You would think they would have been already asked but, here are some questions to ponder regardless of your opinion on the issue;

Why do women have their children taken away in divorce proceedings? The law does not allow for spousal consent to abortion. It is for a woman alone to decide. So, it's her choice, therefor her child. There are extreme circumstances such as abuse, neglect, and abandonment. These are rare because in most cases, the character of the woman is attacked and the ruling tends to focus on that. Without her choice, there is no child. She made the decision so therefor owns the rights to the outcome. Another question would be **why haven't women's groups and advocates argued for this?**

Child care and support are a foreseeable consequence, so why aren't women held responsible? Rights and responsibilities are joined at the hip, you can't have one without the other. Clearly women have the unquestioned right to their child, so they to must have the unquestioned responsibility as well. Since 1973, there have been many women who have raised and supported their children on their own. This alone makes the equality argument that women's groups have been trying to make for years.

Why aren't women paid more than men since they have children to support? It was after World War II that the United States had an interesting dilemma, how to develop a pay scale for both men and women. Most companies opted to pay men more that women because they saw men as "Breadwinners", those who singlehandedly supported the family (wife and children), because women with children stayed home to raise the children. This was not meant to be an unfair or prejudicial practice, but how to spread the payroll dollars to all the employees as they needed them. Since 1973 and the absentee father, women have had the burden of being breadwinners. So why hasn't anyone spoke up to show why women need more money than men?

Why are men required to pay child support? It would seem that a woman made this choice by herself, without any influence. So, if a woman made the choice, then why wouldn't she be obligated to own the outcome? Since that ruling, many women had raised children without a man.

Why are men "Automatically" given rights as a father? Without a woman's choice, there would be no child. The man has nothing to do with this decision, he should own nothing from it. Fatherhood should be a negotiated right. With so many lawyers in congress, it is amazing no one ever thought about a pre-natal agreement. There are pre-nuptial agreements so why not a pre-natal agreement?

It's a common fact that people value things more when they earn them, more than when they are given them. Ask people you know about their first car. Ask was it given to them or did they earn the money to buy it. Most would tell you if it was given to them, it didn't last long. The ones who bought that car probably had it for awhile because, they learned the value and respected it. How much better would society have been if men took pride in being a father, because they had to earn that right?

Why are men and their families allowed to place claims for custody and visitation? Without an agreement in place before hand courts are busy trying to litigate this very issue and, there shouldn't be any right to these people to make a claim. They had nothing to do with the decision for that child to be born, and since the mother holds all rights to the child, there shouldn't be any question on this issue. Yet, our courts are busy with that very question, because the two parties will not address the simplest of facts and put that in writing. They defer to how life used to be before the Roe V Wade ruling and leave the country in legal limbo

Why can't women sell the rights to their child? The law clearly states you can't own or sell a human being, but parents have rights to their children. The children are not property, but to be a parent, you need to have the rights to parent a child. Clearly women have to make a choice to have the child, so they have the rights, all of the rights. So why can't they sell these rights? Why should adoption agencies make all the money from a child who get adopted? This isn't like selling a body part.

Why are mothers allowed to be with their daughters when getting an abortion? It is supposed to be a woman, and a woman alone, without any other person making the decision as to if the child will be born or if the child is to be aborted. We certainly don't let the man who impregnated the woman to be there, so why if a woman who is under the age of 18, or 17 in some states, allowed to choose abortion, and yet their mothers insist on being there. This clearly creates a conflict within the law. The high court was very clear on what they ruled, yet everyday abortions happen and we can only hope there was no "undue influence" as to the woman's choice. Clearly, if **anyone** imposes on the woman's right of choice, and causes death to a fetus, wouldn't they be guilty of homicide? If a woman makes the choice under duress, is it of her own free will?

Why haven't women of color demanded clinics in their neighborhood for women who look like them? It would seem logical that women of color would want what white women have as well. Certainly, if it was a good thing, there would be protests and marches to get equal access to these clinics. As of 2020, no famous woman of color has spoken up to advocate abortion. Many have said they support it, but there is a far cry from support to advocacy. So why won't they advocate? Clearly, there should have been a debate on this issue that includes people of color.

Why hasn't anyone asked these questions in over 40 years? Clearly there have been politicians who have claimed they are for women and stand for women's rights, yet they never thought a woman might want rights to their child. They carry the child for 9 months and it was their choice that the child was not aborted. Why hasn't anyone stood up for a woman's right to make a living wage for herself and her children? Why are tax dollars wasted everyday chasing after men who had no choice in the child being born, and yet we feel they need to pay for the woman's choice? This isn't Legal Fiction, this is a Legal Fantasy, where a choice is made, but not called a choice, unless it is "the Choice" of abortion.

CHAPTER 10

Political Polarization

Clearly this is something most people relate to after the 2016 Presidential election. The polls had Democrat Hillary Rodham-Clinton ahead of Republican Donald Trump in the popular vote. The election results verified the polls because Hillary Rodham-Clinton won the popular vote, but lost where it counts in the Electoral College votes. Since that time, people have been more political in their social media comments. The main stream media was very active in reporting facts and opinion as fact in some cases, but is all of this really the result of that election?

The answer is no. This was something that was coming from state to state. Marijuana has been a hot ticket issue. Some states had voted to allow its use for medical reasons, and other states started to vote to decriminalize it within their state. It was still illegal on a federal level, but states were allowing its citizens to possess small amounts for personal use recreationally. As we have seen, adding a drug to OCCD is gasoline on open flames, this was no different. The question would be how would people behave under the influence of both alcohol and marijuana? As the country was finding out, it made for greater tension between people who didn't like what other side thought, and disliked people based solely on their politics if it didn't echo what they stood for. This left people not just debating ideas, but personally attacking each other.

The debates would start fairly civil, with a disagreeing person maybe making a snide comment about the other person's intellect. Within a few exchanges, these would turn into insults and very ugly comments. Suddenly, it wasn't good enough to be right, you had to rub someone's face in it. Thus, seeing someone else lose an argument was more valuable than winning the argument.

This also led to name calling and poor treatment of others. People were out to find out who was with them and who was against them. This was even in families, were the art of agreeing to disagree became obsolete. It wasn't just people on social media doing this, it was also being done by the main stream media. Imagine being called a name and being stereotyped base solely on who you voted for once.

This polarity led to people refusing to consider new ideas. Whatever ideas they had must be right or they wouldn't have them. New information that didn't support what they thought was considered Fake News. Hopefully we can all see where the OCCD influence is in all of this. Yes, it is good to have you own ideas and opinions, but are they really yours based on who you are and not the Alter Ego version of you? Could your opinions be more about a codependency or need to belong?

When someone responds in insults and not facts, it would be because they have no fact available and if they can intimidate you, they can get you to yield to their way of thinking. It is a form of **Verbal Bullying**. It basically explains much of the behavior I have described. Bullies don't like to being questioned; they insist on being obeyed. Something you can consider when talking to your children about bullying. Seems bullying doesn't end on the playground; it follows you into adult life.

Years ago, people would vote mostly based on their wallets. I ran across a man who echoed that. He claimed when he was in the Navy, he always voted Republican, in his words "because they always voted for pay raises for the military". Then he told me he got out and went to work in a union shop. He joined the union and said he voted Democrat from that point on because Democrats supported unions. Since Roe V Wade, people vote more based on social issues.

This would be a good sign because it means the economy is strong and that is when people look around at the quality of their lives. However, the Roe V Wade influence has left people voting for and supporting things they may not totally be for. It mostly falls into we need people to outnumber the other side, so just go along and we'll get something we want. This was true in the formation of political action committees (PAC). These movements stand for the most part on opposite sides of any argument, but they were formed with the same ideal intent; to show enough voters to sway an election. These are also special interest groups who are looking for something in particular. Where is the line between political activism and OCCD? When your support isn't just to get something you want, but to take something from someone else that they want.

Many people use social media to share their political beliefs. They have a hope that their posts will change someone's political stand, but this really is a fool's errand. They stand as much of a chance to change someone's politics as they do change their religion, or getting them to believe in religion. The best they can hope for is to get some support from others who might believe as they do. Amazingly, they place these posts out for the World to see, and get offended if someone makes a disagreeing comment. Social media can be a brutal playground if you are codependent. Maybe that is why we all vote in a private booth.

There are also those who maintain an unwillingness to admit a mistake in policy. We all have times we think we were right and then as things later unfold, we are proven wrong in our belief. So why would some people refuse to see error in their belief? These people would also be, in many cases, the same people who expect for someone else to see their error in their belief and be expected to abandon their whole system of beliefs. These people will when wrong, make up stories or look for others who have made up stories to prove no matter what, they are right and if necessary, the reset of the World is wrong.

When some people encounter others, who don't agree with them they become offended or insulted. Political beliefs can be very personal and as such, it can be hurtful when others mock those beliefs. In the polarized society, people's feelings are not considered. When people in the main stream media mock people based on who they voted for, creating a whole stereotype based on them, that is at the least offensive, clearly winning the argument is far more important than winning others over to their side. There is a political shaming that happens instead. This is not very effective, if at all, but it seems to be popular and if feeds into the OCCD mindset.

You can read the entire US Constitution and Bill of Rights, and no where within either of them is any provision that allows anyone to silence opposition to any political argument. To the contrary, speech is encouraged. It is political debate that makes us look at our views more closely. It is competition that makes us strive to make a better product at a lower price. We all need each other, especially those who don't agree with us and even those who don't like us. You don't learn much from your friends, because they will withhold certain comments so as not to offend you. It is those who don't know you who will give you a more honest reaction to your statements. How can they speak freely enough to let you know what others truly think if their speech is no longer free? Without totally free speech, you can't have truly free thought. Without free thought, you stifle creativity and new ideas will not make it to the population. This book, for example, could not have been written and the diagnosis would never be presented to the public, if freedom of speech is limited to only what some people want to hear.

All we as individuals can do is be open-minded. Give others the space they need to express their ideas. You don't have to agree with everything you hear, nor do you have to feel like an outcast if you don't. We are all created differently, and as long as we remain teachable, we can look forward to others agreeing with us, even if we choose not to agree with the popular ideas.

CHAPTER 11

Summation

Like everything in life, good or bad, all things must come to an end. So too must this book. I started out explaining I'm not the guy you would think of to speak on this topic. I came across it honestly enough, just not what people would expect from me. Perhaps that is why I was so effective in finding this disorder. When you go off the beaten path, you don't have rules and expectations that have to be honored. Maybe others will find this book interesting enough to research this area and find something else that will help us all. That really is my hope, to inspire others to help solve some of society's problems.

I have shown where this is a truly different disorder. As we looked at the disorders, we could see some were close, but lacked something to show it fit for this purpose. Science has given us many great discoveries, and our lives are better for them. It took an openness to find this disorder and discipline to learn how to define it. Treatments for this disorder can certainly come from the scientific community. I will move on to gather my notes and write a second book on this topic. Clearly, we have adults who lack the skill set of an adult in social situations. My next book will address that because, unfortunately, addicts/alcoholics have the mind of an adult, but the social maturity of a toddler. Sounds like a teenager, doesn't it?

I tried to make this book unique in that you get to see many different applications of this disorder and can see the damage it can cause. The life of an addict/alcoholic is just the start. We also need to know they come from a family. At some point in their lives they had good friends and neighbors. This disorder effects more than just one person, because it takes a village to raise a child. We must also recognize the village and the impact it left on them. This disorder isn't just a name to attach, it has a definition that gives a person some idea what it is. Too often people throw out insults without a real basis of fact on them. This disorder explains why a person behaves the way they do and what others around them are going through.

I've also explained how this disorder drives an addiction, or anti-social behavior. How then also this disorder will manifest itself into a lifestyle or life-long disability. How it can attract other problems, and how it also creates victims. Sometimes people are lucky enough to get out of the way, and other times they are stuck in its path. As some will always have distain for an addict/alcoholic, perhaps this book will open their eyes to the people who get hurt and the other lives it damages.

Another goal I had for this book was to show how others were hurt also. Too often, we focus on the individual with the problem and forget they have/had parents, maybe siblings, aunts, uncles, cousins, etc. We also forget the neighbors, co-workers, and those who put up their behavior. There are more victims than we first see, and I thought it was about time not only to recognize them, but also to show that they too have been suffering with the same disorder.

With so many being either directly effected or indirectly effected, there should be more dialog about these problems. The big question is why hasn't there been? There is a phrase, "Elephant in the room". It refers to everyone knowing something is there, but no one pointing it out. This thing can be rather large, and still no one will talk about it. Hopefully, this book can remove that elephant and we can all start a discussion. I have tried to give knowledge on this topic so everyone can discuss this topic with some knowledge, and certainly some background. Information without an application is trivia. Information with an application is knowledge. I hope you can show much knowledge on this topic!

There is a sequel to this book. It was a very natural endeavor. I had to use some different techniques to isolate this disorder. In doing so, I found people with this disorder lacking in some social areas. The real challenge is to provide those who are suffering with this disorder the information they need to be a complete person without giving them too much where they could use it to further control others. I have found a way to do that. In addition, the same book would help those who have been controlled and see no escape from it. It will be in a workbook form, but can also be used to have discussion topics within a meeting for a support group.

I hope you have enjoyed this book and will tell others. It takes at least one person to raise a topic before a discussion can begin. I hope you will be that person and will find things not in this book to shine a light of discovery on yourself!

About the Author

Wolfgang Schultz spent almost thirty years in the Professional Wrestling field. He worked as a Wrestler, Trainer, and Promoter. He held the World Heavyweight Title for both the International Wrestling Organization (IWO), as well as the Monarch Wrestling Mecca (MWM). He also worked for many other promotions too numerous to mention.

While in Professional Wrestling, Wolfgang also did many appearances outside the ring. These appearances were directly related to child health and welfare. Such as hosting health fairs and making school visits. He also visited children in several hospitals across the country. He also gave talks regarding Bullying and the importance of education. His motto for years was "Say no to gangs, drugs, and violence.".